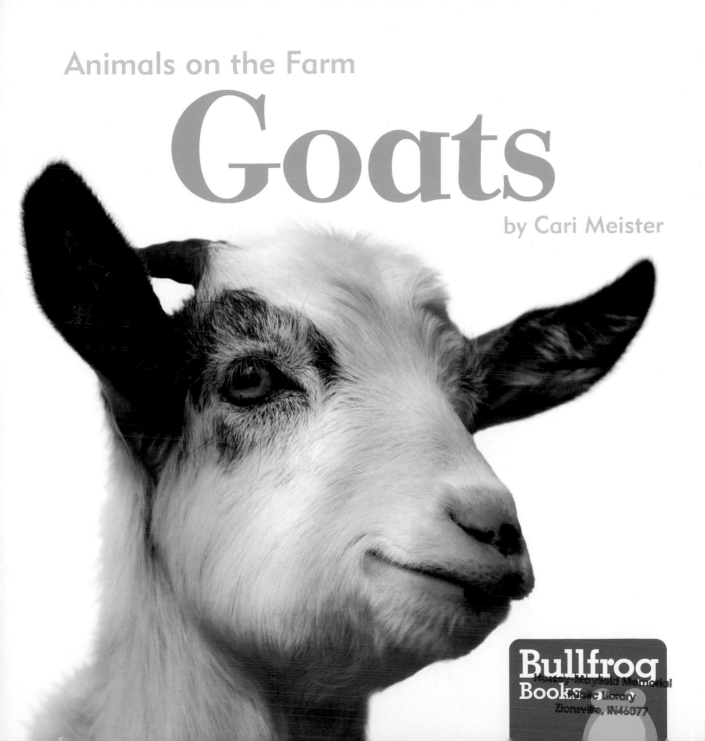

Animals on the Farm

Goats

by Cari Meister

Ideas for Parents and Teachers

Bullfrog Books let children practice reading nonfiction at the earliest levels. Repetition, familiar words, and photos support early readers. Here are some tips for reading with children.

Before Reading

- Discuss the cover photo with the children. What does it tell them?

- Look at the picture glossary together. Read and discuss the words.

Read the Book

- "Walk" through the book and look at the photos. Let the children ask questions.

- Read the book to the children, or have them read independently.

After Reading

- Prompt them to think more. Ask: Would you like to have a goat? Why or why not? Would you like to try some goat cheese?

Bullfrog Books are published by Jump!
5357 Penn Avenue South
Minneapolis, MN 55419
www.jumplibrary.com

Library of Congress Cataloging-in-Publication Data
Meister, Cari.
  Goats / by Cari Meister.
    p. cm. -- (Bullfrog books: Animals on the farm)
  Includes index.
  Summary: "Goats narrate this photo-illustrated book describing the body parts and behavior of goats on a farm. Includes picture glossary"-- Provided by publisher.
  ISBN 978-1-62031-003-8 (hardcover)
  1. Goats--Juvenile literature. 2. Goats--Behavior--Juvenile literature. I. Title.
  SF383.35.M45 2013
  636.3'9--dc23
                              2012008224

Photo Credits: All photos by Dreamstime except: Alamy, 16-17; Getty, 6–7, 12, 12–13, 14–15, 18; iStock, 10; Shutterstock, 3b, 17, 20–21, 24; Superstock, 8

Series Editor: Rebecca Glaser
Series Designer: Ellen Huber
Production: Chelsey Luther

Printed in the United States of America at Corporate Graphics in North Mankato, Minnesota
7-2012/ PO 1121
10 9 8 7 6 5 4 3 2 1

Table of Contents

Goats on the Farm

I am a goat.
I live on a farm.
Have you ever
seen a goat?

Do you see my
floppy ears?
They keep
out dust.

hoof

Do you see my hard hooves? They need to be trimmed.

Do you see
my soft lips?

They help
me eat hay.

pupil

Do you see my eye?
My pupil is a rectangle.
It helps me see at night.

Do you see my teeth?

14

My baby teeth
fell out.

15

Do you see
her udder?

It gives milk.

The farmer
takes her milk.

He makes
cheese.

Do you see
my horns?

I use them to fight and play.

19

I won!

I am king of the hill!

Parts of a Goat

horns
Hard, bony growths on a goat's head.

ears
Body parts used for hearing; some goats have floppy ears.

hoof
The hard outer covering of an animal's foot.

Picture Glossary

cheese
A food made from milk. Goat cheese is very soft.

trim
To cut off small pieces of something.

pupil
The black part of a goat's eye that lets in light.

udder
The baglike part of a female goat that makes milk.

Index

To Learn More

Learning more is as easy as 1, 2, 3.

1) Go to www.factsurfer.com

2) Enter "goat" into the search box.

3) Click the "Surf" button to see a list of websites.

With factsurfer.com, finding more information is just a click away.

6/14